THEN & NOW
SHEFFIELD

Alistair Lofthouse

© Alistair Lofthouse 1999

Printed and published by:
ALD Design & Print
279 Sharrow Vale Road
Sheffield S11 8ZF

Telephone 0114 267 9402
E:mail a.lofthouse@btinternet.com

Typeset by Andrew Billingham.

ISBN 1-901587-07-X

First Published 1999
Second Edition 2001

Other titles in the series:

Mi-Amigo - The Story of Sheffield's Flying Fortress - David Harvey	ISBN 1-901587-00-2
Tales From a Peak District Bookshop - Mike Smith	ISBN 1-901587-01-0
Tha' Don't look Proper - Anne Hunt	ISBN 1-901587-02-9
Shiny Sheff - The Story of Sheffield's Fighting Ships - Alistair Lofthouse	ISBN 1-901587-03-7
Doug's War - An Erksome Business - Doug Sanderson	ISBN 1-901587-04-5
The Dramatic Story of The Sheffield Flood - Peter Machan	ISBN 1-901584-05-3
Carl Wark - Peak District Fortress or Folly? - Mick Savage	ISBN 1-901587-06-1
Charlie Peace, The Banner Cross Murderer - Peter Machan	ISBN 1-901587-08-8
Then & Now - The Sheffield Blitz - Alistair Lofthouse	ISBN 1-901587-09-6
They Lived in Sharrow and Nether Edge - Nether Edge Neighbourhood Group	ISBN 1-901587-10-X
Discovering Derbyshire's White Peak - Tom Bates	ISBN 1-901587-11-8
Lost Sheffield - Portrait of a Victorian City - Peter Machan	ISBN 1-901587-12-6
The Sheffield Flood - Large format for schools - Peter Machan	ISBN 1-901587-13-4
The Sheffield Outrages, The Trade Union Scandals - Peter Machan	ISBN 1-901587-14-2
A Layman's Look at the History, Industry, People and Places of Oughtibridge Worrall and Wharncliffe Side - Doug Sanderson	ISBN 1-901587-15-0

Introduction

I find looking at old photographs of my local environment interesting. However, very often I find myself wondering where a particular scene was or what location the photograph was taken from.

My idea, which is far from original, was to attempt to retake the same photograph that was taken, in many cases, over one hundred years ago. I have attempted to locate the exact position of the original photographer. In some cases trees or buildings have been in the way and I hope the reader can forgive me for not risking my life, standing in the middle of busy roads, which would have been necessary in a few cases.

Some pictures show vast changes, some show remarkably few. I hope they are all of interest.

Alistair Lofthouse

Acknowledgements

Where possible, permission has been gained for use of these photographs but, in a number of cases, the originators have been untraceable. Apologies are now made for those I could not trace through the mist of time. I am grateful, however, to Dorothy Smith, Kenneth Atkin, R. Jenkinson, Peter Machan and the Friends of the Botanical Gardens Society.

St. Paul's Church, Pinstone Street

Demolished in the 1930's to make way for the Peace Gardens.
The name 'Peace Gardens' was only formally recognised some 30 years later.

Town Hall Square from Barkers Pool

*The Regent became the Gaumont before being rebuilt in 1985 in its controversial style.
As the Odeon, its final closure came ten years later.*

Barker's Pool

*Named after the pool originally situated here which provided some of Sheffield's water supply,
Barkers Pool was opened weekly in order to flush the streets of rubbish and manure.
The new Coles building, ahead of its time, was built on the site of the old Albert Hall.*

High Street

Much of High Street was destroyed during the war. What was the Midland Bank survives today as a pub. It is interesting to note that here the modern trams follow exactly the same route as the old ones.

West Street c.1910

The Royal Hospital is prominent in the background. This hospital, along with the Royal Infirmary, was superceded by the Hallamshire Hospital in 1978.
Demolished in 1980 much of the old Royal Hospital site is still a rough car park today.

West Street

The tram lines went in 1960 only to come back in 1993.

Fargate

Note, the Yorkshire Bank still remains today in the same location.

Fargate

Shown here in 1886 before the trams.
The cobbles reappeared in 1997, although in the Italian style.

The Moor

Today, looking up the Moor, only the Town Hall still remains of the original buildings, most having en destroyed during the blitz of December 1940. The German air force targeted Sheffield's industrial heartland, but most of the bombs fell on the City Centre.
Today's Moor is very much in the 50's post war style and was pedestrianised in 1979.

Northends, West Street

The blitz of december 1940 saw long establised printers Northends receive a direct hit. Both company and building have survived, however, Northends moved to much larger premises at Heeley in the late 1980's. The building became a pub, initially Barkers but later Edwards. A smaller traditional pub, The Red Lion, was eventually knocked through to the new pub.

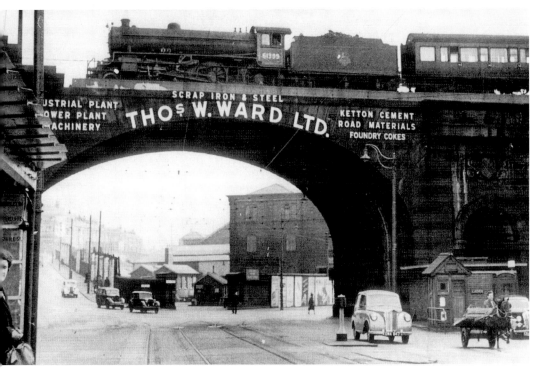

Wicker Arches

One of Sheffield's landmarks, the Wicker Arches were built in the 1850's to carry the Sheffield to Manchester railway line. Sheffield Victoria Station was situated to the top right of the photograph and closed in 1969. Passenger services stopped in the late 1960's with freight lasting until 1983.

Saville Street

The goods yard went as freight moved from rail to road. It is a little ironic that the site is now a car dealership. Only the gate posts remain of the goods yard today.

Victoria Station

Today The Royal Victoria Hotel, a Holiday Inn, remains as a link with past railways. Although Victoria Station closed in 1969 the station buildings were gradually demolished over a long period of time ending in 1985. Only the wall to the right remains recognisable today.

Mappin Art Gallery

Bombed during the War losing a number of paintings, the damaged section was later rebuilt. Today the park entrance provides an emergency helicopter landing pad for the Childrens' hospital across the road.

The University of Sheffield, Western Bank

Since its foundation, the University of Sheffield has always maintained a position of one of Britain's top Universities. The term 'Red Brick' is very much in evidence in both old and new photographs.

Hunter's Bar

The water trough on the island was provided for passing horses by the Wilson family, famed snuff manufacturers, having their factory at the top of Sharrow Vale Road. When the roundabout was built the trough was moved to a field in Mayfield Valley. Eventually it may end up at the restored Botanical Gardens.

Hunter's Bar

Once a toll road to Chapel-en-le-Frith. Where the roundabout is now once stood a toll house and gate where tolls were paid to use the road. The gate posts became the entrance to Endcliffe Park, but were later relocated onto the roundabout in a similar, but not exact, position.

Rustlings Road

*Only the trees and methods of transport have changed in this scene.
The trams were withdrawn from Rustlings Road in January 1952.*

Botanical Gardens

*The covered passages that joined these three Victorian conservatories were removed in 1906.
Although boarded up today, they await the start of the £3 million restoration programme which
will restore the gardens to their former glory of over one hundred years ago.*

Botanical Gardens

The bandstand has long since gone.

Endcliffe Park

Recent plans to convert the park ranger station and house to a café have failed.

Endcliffe Park

Yet another bandstand gone. Sadly this photo does not show the café that narrowly escaped destruction in February 1944 when an American B-17 Flying Fortress, Mi-Amigo, crashed just a few metres behind it. All ten airmen died, but there were no injuries on the ground. The story of Mi-Amigo has been published in a book written by Sheffield Historian David Harvey.

Endcliffe Park

The boating lake was once the source of water that powered the water wheel located in the mill building in the background. Today the lake is heavily silted, the boats and building having long since gone.

Glenalmond Road, Banner Cross

The clutter of today's transport marks the main contrast at Banner Cross today.
The wooded hill in the far background had yet to be built upon.

Kenwood, Sharrow

The lodge to the right provided an entrance to Kenwood Park, now the Swallow Hotel.
The gas lamp survived on an enlarged roundabout until the early 1980's.

Machon Bank

There are no landmarks left to properly identify this photograph, the direction of the road being the only clue.

Nether Edge

The tram terminus was situated just behind the camera position.
This particular tram route was the first to close.

Sheaf Bank, Heeley

Much has changed since this 1950's photo.
It is hard to imagine that this was once a busy shopping centre.

Chesterfield Road, Heeley

With various uses the Heeley Picture Palace lasted until it was destroyed by fire in the early 1980's

Norfolk Park Lodge

The entrance to Norfolk Park remains today almost unchanged.

Meersbrook Park Road

Car parking was not a problem in this earlier scene.

Millhouses Terminus

The turning circle in front of the shops remained for many years after the trams disappeared in 1960. Retained to allow buses to turn round, it became rarely used resulting in the land being sold off in the early 1990's enabling the building of a block of retirement flats.

Millhouses Engine Sheds

Once the home for 100 steam engines of the London Midland Scottish Railway. The end of steam in the 60's led to the engine sheds being taken over by Jacobs tools. The rest of the site remained unused until Tesco built their new superstore and car park on the site in 1996.

Millhouses & Ecclesall Station

Taken from the bridge that crosses the railway at Millhouses, this photograph shows another victim of the 1960's railway decline. The station buildings remained until 1970. One wonders today whether Supertram could occupy the space left by the local lines to the left of the picture.

Dore & Totley Station

By the 1970's only local trains to Manchester stopped at this station and during the mid 1980's most of the station was demolished. The ticket office to the right was used by a printing firm and is now an Indian restaurant.

Totley Rise

The original road became the service road to the shops when the road was widened to a dual carriageway.

Hare & Hounds, Dore Village

The rural charm of Dore Village very much survives today. The building in the foreground has, however, made way for the entrance to the Hare & Hounds pub car park.

Dore

The little cottage in the centre remains virtually unchanged, The Devonshire Arms pub is now located to the left of the picture and houses now cover the farmland to the distance.

Millhouses Lane

Very much a rural scene around sixty years ago. The houses on the left gave way to the Ecclesall tram terminus. Alledgedlya tram once ran away and hit the house in the middle of the picture.

Bents Green

Once a tiny village, now the suburbs of south-west Sheffield. The cottages in the distance are the only recognisable buildings left here.

Lodge Moor Hospital

Once an isolation hospital, hence its somewhat isolated position. The last iron lung was inserted here in the 1970's. Closed in 1995 the site awaits development into housing.

Crosspool

Most of the buildings exist today, but now as retail properties.

Manchester Road, Crosspool

The Crosspool Tavern to the left has been totally rebuilt.

Manchester Road

Taken on a quiet day, this scene remains almost timeless.

Nether Green Tram Terminus

Nether Green terminus joined the lines tram routes from Broomhill and Hunter's Bar.
The Broomhill branch along Fulwood Road was one of the first to close in August 1936.

Nether Green Tram Terminus

The Nether Green to Hunter's Bar tram route closed in 1952.
The motor car now clearly dominates this scene.

Whiteley Woods Boating Lake

Situated in what is now Bingham Park, the pond supplied water to power the Ibbotson Wheel for the manufacture of files. In 1902 the wheel was still in operation, but now only the pond exists. Shepherd Wheel is just located just a few hundred yards upstream and remains preserved intact.

Bingham Park

The building on the left appears to be from the 1920's.

Oakbrook Road, Nether Green

The Council once planned a roundabout at the junction of Hangingwater Road and Oakbrook Road. A strip of land, off to the left of the photograph on Nethergreen Road was purchased to allow road widening, but the plans never went ahead.

Fulwood Road, Ranmoor

This row of shops was built to supply the expanding population of Ranmoor over one hundred years ago and remains remarkably unaltered today.

Ranmoor

The Bull's Head pub, on the left, was originally called the Highland Laddie.

Brookhouse Hill, Fulwood

Looking up to the bottom of Crimicar Lane, long before the shops were built.

Commonside, Walkley

Apparently, shop sun-blinds are not so popular these days.

York Street

Boarded up and ready for demolition this building's replacement was built, fortunately, following the style of its neighbour.

Park Square

Many of the photographs in this book are around one hundred years old. To end I've included a picture I took as a student in 1985. I feel it shows that Sheffield is still constantly changing, Hyde Park flats having gone and Supertram having arrived.